Journey to Freedom

ROSA PARKS

BY L. S. SUMMER

"PEOPLE ALWAYS SAY THAT I DIDN'T GIVE UP MY SEAT BECAUSE I WAS TIRED, BUT THAT ISN'T TRUE. I WAS NOT TIRED PHYSICALLY, OR NO MORE TIRED THAN I USUALLY WAS AT THE END OF A WORKING DAY. I WAS NOT OLD, ALTHOUGH SOME PEOPLE HAVE AN IMAGE OF ME AS BEING OLD THEN. I WAS FORTY-TWO. NO, THE ONLY TIRED I WAS, WAS TIRED OF GIVING IN."

~ ROSA PARKS *(ROSA PARKS: MY STORY)* ~

Cover and page 4 caption:
Rosa Parks smiling after the
Supreme Court ruled Alabama
bus segregation was illegal in
December of 1956

Content Consultant:
David J. Garrow, PhD, U.S.
historian and Pulitzer Prize-
winning author of Bearing
the Cross: Martin Luther
King, Jr., and the Southern
Christian Leadership
Conference

Published in the United States of America by The Child's World®
1980 Lookout Drive, Mankato, MN 56003-1705
800-599-READ • www.childsworld.com

ACKNOWLEDGEMENTS

The Child's World®: Mary Berendes, Publishing Director

The Design Lab: Kathleen Petelinsek, Design; Gregory Lindholm, Page Production

Red Line Editorial: Holly Saari, Editorial Direction

PHOTOS

Cover and page 4: Bettmann/Corbis

Interior: AP Images, 7, 16, 17, 21, 23, 24; Bettmann/Corbis, 6, 27; Corbis, 12; Dick DeMarsico/
Library of Congress, 9; Gene Herrick/AP Images, 19, 20, 22; Horace Cort/AP Images, 14; Hulton
Archive/Staff/Getty Images, 11; John Vachon/Library of Congress, 5; Paul Sancya/AP Images, 25;
William Philpott/Reuters/Corbis, 26

LIBRARY OF CONGRESS CATALOGING-IN-PUBLICATION DATA

Summer, L. S., 1959–

  Rosa Parks / by L. S. Summer.

    p. cm. — (Journey to freedom)

  Includes bibliographical references and index.

  ISBN 978-1-60253-133-8 (library bound : alk. paper)

  1. Parks, Rosa, 1913–2005—Juvenile literature. 2. African American women—Alabama—
Montgomery—Biography—Juvenile literature. 3. African Americans—Alabama—Montgomery—
Biography—Juvenile literature. 4. Civil rights workers—Alabama—Montgomery—Biography—
Juvenile literature. 5. African Americans—Civil rights—Alabama—Montgomery—Juvenile
literature. 6. Segregation in transportation—Alabama—Montgomery—History—20th century—
Juvenile literature. 7. Montgomery (Ala.)—Race relations—Juvenile literature. 8. Montgomery
(Ala.)—Biography—Juvenile literature. I. Title. II. Series.

  F334.M753P388 2009

  323.092—dc22

  [B]

                                      2008031937

CONTENTS

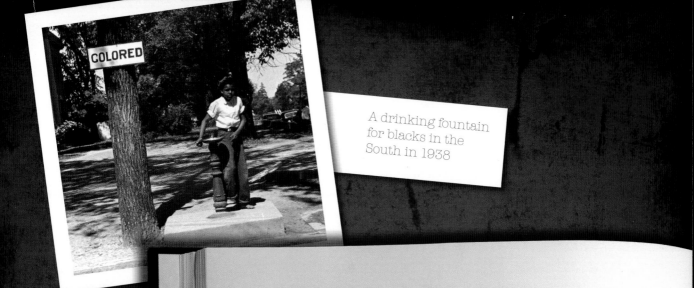

A drinking fountain for blacks in the South in 1938

Chapter One

A DIFFERENT TIME

he United States in the 1950s was very different than it is today. People of different skin colors were less likely to play, eat, or work together. In the South, white and black people were separated in public places. This system was called **segregation**. It prohibited whites and blacks from such things as swimming in the same pools and drinking from the same water fountains. Public facilities had signs that read "Whites Only" and "Colored Only."

Black people were freed from slavery after the U.S. Civil War in the 1860s. However, they did not immediately gain the same rights as whites. **Racism** and **discrimination** continued to play a strong role in the treatment of black people. Blacks usually

Rosa Parks speaking to an interviewer before her court trial

The rules that enabled segregation were called "Jim Crow laws." These laws made discrimination against blacks legal.

lived in the worst parts of town. Black children received little or no education. Life was especially difficult for blacks in the South. Laws were created to keep blacks and whites separated. Sometimes blacks were targets of violence, including **lynching**.

Many people felt segregation laws were wrong. Black people wanted the same rights as white people. They wanted to be treated fairly and respectfully. Because of this, groups formed to work for black civil rights. Citizens started to demonstrate against the unfair rules.

In 1955, a 42-year-old, black seamstress named Rosa Parks took an important action that set change in motion. Her simple act—the act of saying no—became one of the major milestones on the road to equal rights for blacks in the United States.

Chapter Two

GROWING UP

 osa Louise McCauley was born on February 4, 1913, in Tuskegee, Alabama, to James and Leona McCauley. Her mother was a well-educated schoolteacher. Her father was a carpenter who left the family when Rosa was a little girl. After James left, Leona and her two children, Rosa and Sylvester, moved back to Leona's family farm in Pine Level, Alabama, to live with Rosa's grandparents.

The only teaching job Leona could find was in another town. Leona worked and lived there during the week and went home for the weekends. When her mother was gone, Rosa spent a lot of time with her grandparents. From them, she learned the importance of education. She also developed a strong faith in God. She was taught that all people deserve fair treatment regardless of their skin color. These values remained important to Rosa throughout her life.

When Rosa was a young girl, her mother taught her how to read. Rosa loved books. She also enjoyed going to school. She attended an all-black elementary school with about 60 students. Rosa spent only five months a year in class because her elementary school was closed during harvest time. During the harvest, black children had to help pick cotton. White children did not have to work in the fields and attended school for nine months of the year.

When Rosa was 11 years old, she went to a private school named Montgomery Industrial School. The school was founded for black girls. The teachers at the Montgomery Industrial School taught their students the importance of dignity and self-respect. They encouraged the girls to set goals. They inspired their students to believe in themselves. Rosa loved the school and was an excellent student. She worked hard to earn money for tuition by cleaning classrooms in her spare time.

Some people did not approve of blacks being educated. The Montgomery Industrial School was set on fire twice and was finally forced to close. Rosa then attended a teacher's college in Montgomery, Alabama, that operated a school for black children. At this school, black students could study for nine months. Before Rosa

Rosa wrote in her autobiography:
"What I learned best at Miss White's school was that I was a person with dignity and self-respect, and I should not set my sights lower than anybody else just because I was black."

Students saying the Pledge of Allegiance in a school for black children

graduated, her mother and grandmother became ill. She chose to leave school after tenth grade and moved to Pine Level, Alabama, to care for them.

When Rosa was 16 years old, her grandmother died. Even though her mother's health improved, Rosa decided to stay in Pine Level. Her family needed her to manage the farm.

Soon, Rosa met a young man named Raymond Parks. Raymond shared many of Rosa's values. He did not believe in letting whites treat him unfairly. He also believed that blacks should have the same rights as whites.

Raymond and Rosa had similar experiences growing up. Raymond's father was in the building trade and left his family when Raymond was young. Education was important to Raymond. His mother taught him at home, as he could not attend the local school because he was black. Raymond also cared for his mother when she became ill.

Raymond and Rosa fell in love. They were married in her mother's home in Pine Level on December 18, 1932. Raymond encouraged Rosa to finish high school. In 1934, she received her diploma.

Chapter Three

SEGREGATION IN THE SOUTH

The Constitution promises important rights to U.S. citizens. These rights include the freedom of speech and the freedom of religion. Citizens also have the right to vote. These are called civil rights. Unfortunately, black people have not always had these rights.

Segregation in the South allowed a strict separation between blacks and whites. Black children could not attend the same schools as white children. Black families could not eat in white restaurants. They could not see movies in white theaters. In Montgomery, whites and blacks could not even play cards, checkers, or dominoes together.

A woman recruiting members for the NAACP

Founded in 1909, the NAACP is the nation's oldest civil rights organization.

Soon after Rosa and Raymond married, the young couple moved to Montgomery. This is where they learned about the National Association for the Advancement of Colored People (NAACP). This organization played an important role in the **civil rights movement**. The NAACP worked to help black people gain fair treatment under the law.

In 1943, Rosa became a part of the civil rights movement. She joined the Montgomery chapter of the NAACP. She was elected secretary and assisted the chapter's president, E. D. Nixon. Rosa and Raymond devoted much of their time and energy to the organization. They hoped they could make a change in how blacks were treated in the South. One cause they felt strongly about was the right to vote.

Like other U.S. citizens, all blacks legally held the right to vote. In order to vote, a person had to register with the government. In the South, whites tried to keep blacks from registering. Sometimes they threatened black people who tried to register. Other times, they simply turned them away. Rosa tried to register three times before she was finally successful. In 1945, Rosa was registered, yet had to pay a poll tax in order to vote. After that, she voted in every election until her death.

Blacks also were treated unfairly on public buses, which had segregation rules. Blacks were often threatened or shamed when riding the buses. On Montgomery buses, blacks had to enter through the back door. The fare box, however, was in the front. Blacks had to use the front door to enter and pay their fare. Then they had to get off the bus, walk to the back door, and board the bus again.

The bus company employed only white drivers. Many of them were unkind or even cruel to blacks. Sometimes, bus drivers pulled away before black passengers reached the back door—even after they had paid their fare.

One day in 1943, after she was turned away from registering to vote, Rosa boarded a bus at the front door

Some blacks were freed from slavery after President Abraham Lincoln signed the Emancipation Proclamation. Two presidential orders, the first in 1862 and the second in 1863, freed slaves in areas of the Confederacy that were still fighting against the Union.

A view of a segregated bus, with whites seated in the front and blacks in the back

and paid her fare. The bus was very crowded. Blacks who were forced to stand blocked the rear doorway. Rosa realized there was not a good reason to get off the bus and walk to the back door. She would have to struggle to push her way through the entry. Instead, she turned down the aisle and walked directly to the back of the bus.

The bus driver ordered her to exit and enter again through the back door. Rosa patiently explained that she was already on the bus. She saw no need to get off. The driver ordered her to do as he said or get off the bus altogether. Rosa did not move.

The driver rose from his seat and walked back to where Rosa stood. He threatened her and angrily pulled on her coat sleeve. Rosa knew that he had a gun. She decided to get off the bus and wait for the next one.

Twelve years later, in 1955, segregation continued on Alabama buses. The bus drivers were required by law to enforce segregated seating. Each bus operated by Montgomery City Lines, Inc. had 36 seats. The ten seats in the front were reserved for whites only. Even if whites were not on the bus, blacks could not sit in the front seats. The ten seats in the back of the bus were reserved for blacks only. Blacks could sit in the middle seats only if whites did not want them. Bus drivers carried weapons to make sure people did as they were told. They also had the help of police if they needed it. Not many people dared to challenge the segregation rules. If they did, they might end up in jail.

On December 1, 1955, Rosa boarded a Montgomery bus and sat down in one of the middle seats. Three other black people sat in the same row. A white man boarded the bus after all the seats were taken. The driver told all four blacks in Rosa's row to stand up so that the white man could sit down. The other three seats had to remain empty. Blacks and whites could not sit together in the same row.

The three others got up, but Rosa stayed in her seat. She knew this was one way that whites tried to make blacks feel inferior, and she was tired of it. She was not going to get up. The bus driver told her again to give up her seat. Rosa simply said no. The driver said he was going to call the police. Two police officers arrested Rosa and took her to jail. She cooperated and stayed calm throughout the humiliating process. Rosa was charged with violating the laws of segregation. She asked a police officer why they treated black people so badly. He said he did not know. He was only following the law.

A bus diagram showing where Rosa Parks was sitting when she was told to move

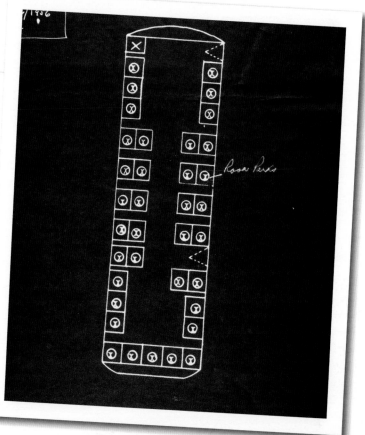

Chapter Four

THE BEGINNING OF CHANGE

The decision by Rosa Parks to stay seated showed other blacks that they could protest unfair rules. Rosa's protest caused the civil rights movement to become more active. Because of this, she is often called the "mother of the civil rights movement."

Several important things resulted from Rosa's arrest. The first was the Montgomery Bus **Boycott**. Before Rosa's trial, a group called the Women's Political Council called for action. They passed out more than 20,000 flyers asking blacks to stay off the buses on December 5, the day of the trial, even if they had to miss a day of school or work. Word quickly spread.

Before Rosa, other blacks had been arrested for disobeying bus segregation rules. The Montgomery Bus Boycott was prompted by Rosa's arrest, however, because she was previously involved in the civil rights movement and was a well-respected citizen.

Not one black person rode the bus in Montgomery on December 5, 1955. Some people walked or rode bikes wherever they needed to go. Others took taxis with black drivers who charged only the price of a bus ride. Blacks who owned cars shuttled others back and forth throughout the day.

At her trial on December 5, Rosa was found guilty of violating segregation laws and fined $14. This was the **verdict** E. D. Nixon and the NAACP wanted. If a U.S. citizen is found guilty of a crime, he or she can ask a higher court to reconsider the verdict. Rosa and the NAACP then had the opportunity to take Montgomery's bus segregation law to the nation's most important court. The NAACP leaders planned to **appeal** Rosa's case before the Supreme Court. This was the second important result of Rosa's arrest. A year earlier, the Supreme Court had decided that it was illegal to have segregated schools. The NAACP leaders hoped the higher court would decide that bus segregation was also wrong.

After Rosa's trial, Montgomery's black leaders held a meeting. They wanted to discuss if their community should continue the boycott. Every seat in the building was filled. Hundreds of people stood outside. Several people made speeches, including two local pastors named Ralph Abernathy and Martin Luther King Jr. The decision was made to continue the boycott until the bus segregation rules ended.

Blacks refused to ride Montgomery buses for 381 days—more than one year. The city's white citizens tried many things to end the boycott, including threats and acts of violence. But blacks did not give in. For more than one year, black people with cars gave others rides to their destinations. Many people traveled on foot.

The Montgomery police arrested many of the boycotters. Rosa was arrested a second time, this time for participating in the boycott. Rosa, King, and other leaders gave many speeches during the Montgomery Bus Boycott. They talked about the boycott and the unfairness of the South's segregation laws.

On November 13, 1956, the Supreme Court made its decision about Montgomery bus segregation. It ruled that Montgomery had to **integrate** its public bus lines. The bus company's segregation rules were now illegal. By December 21, blacks were free to choose where they sat on a bus. White bus drivers could no longer use the law to treat black passengers badly. This was the third important result of Rosa's arrest. More important perhaps, blacks learned that they had the power to change things. When blacks united as a community, they could improve their own lives and those of blacks across the country.

Brown v. Board of Education of Topeka *was a landmark court case decided in 1954. Supreme Court justices ruled that segregation in schools was no longer legal.*

Martin Luther King Jr. is perhaps the most widely known leader of the civil rights movement. He favored nonviolent protests as a way for blacks to gain civil rights. In 1964, he was awarded the Nobel Peace Prize for his actions.

The Supreme Court decision against bus segregation could not be ignored. Unfortunately, many whites continued to believe in segregation. Some white people threatened those who had been involved in the bus boycott. The homes of King and Nixon were bombed. Rosa and Raymond received threatening phone calls. Rosa's mother now lived with them. Some nights, she would talk to friends on the phone all night to keep the threatening calls from coming in. The Parks family was afraid. Raymond kept a gun near him when he slept at night.

Many blacks lost their jobs during and after the boycott. Soon Rosa and Raymond were also out of work. They decided it was time to leave Montgomery. Rosa's brother Sylvester lived in Detroit, Michigan. In 1957, they moved there as well.

Rosa was arrested and fingerprinted for her involvement in the bus boycott.

Two black men sat in the front seats of a Montgomery bus on December 21, 1956, the day the city buses were integrated.

Montgomery Bus Boycott leaders Ralph Abernathy (left), Martin Luther King Jr. (center), and Bayard Rustin (right) attended the boycott trial.

Rosa had become well known. She did not let moving to Detroit stop her from being active in the civil rights movement. She traveled around the country to speak about her experiences and to urge equality and justice. Meanwhile, King, Abernathy, and others had formed a new organization. They called it the Southern Christian Leadership Conference (SCLC). Its goal was to use nonviolent **civil disobedience** as a way to gain civil rights. Rosa was a supporter of the SCLC and continued to work toward making positive changes in the lives of blacks.

Martin Luther King Jr. spoke to a large crowd at the Lincoln Memorial during the March on Washington.

Chapter Five

POST-BOYCOTT ACTION

he case of Rosa Parks and the Montgomery Bus Boycott helped launch the civil rights movement. Soon, there were other boycotts. Blacks marched in large groups throughout the South to demand better treatment. They organized freedom rides to integrate bus travel between states.

In 1963, approximately 250,000 people participated in a protest march in Washington DC. At the time, the March on Washington was the largest demonstration in the history of the nation's capital. One main point of the event was to demonstrate that all blacks should be treated fairly and have equal civil rights.

During the March on Washington, Martin Luther King Jr. gave his famous "I Have a Dream" speech at the Lincoln Memorial.

President Lyndon Johnson reached to shake Martin Luther King Jr.'s hand after signing the Civil Rights Act in 1964.

On July 2, 1964, President Lyndon Johnson signed the Civil Rights Act. It made all segregation illegal. Now the U.S. government would stand up for the civil rights of its black citizens. But the new law could not instantly change people's beliefs or behavior. Blacks still faced discrimination. Rosa Parks knew there was much more to be done.

In 1965, Rosa became an assistant to a black congressman, Representative John Conyers of Michigan. Rosa respected his views and ideas. She worked for Conyers until she retired in 1988.

The 1970s brought difficult times for Rosa. Raymond died in 1977. Her brother Sylvester died three months later. Rosa's mother moved to a nursing home because her health continued to fail. Rosa visited her mother three times each day. In 1978, Rosa moved her mother back home to care for her. Her mother died the following year.

In 1987, Rosa and her close friend Elaine Steele founded the Rosa and Raymond Parks Institute for Self Development. The organization offers education and community programs to young people between the ages of 11 and 18. Youth education was always very important to Rosa. The organization also awards scholarships to black students.

Vice President Al Gore with Rosa after she was awarded the Congressional Gold Medal in 1999.

One program at the institute is called Pathways to Freedom. Children in the program have the chance to travel across the United States tracing the path of the **Underground Railroad**. They also visit the scenes of important events in the civil rights movement.

Rosa received many awards and honors for her work in civil rights. Some of these include the Eleanor Roosevelt Women of Courage Award (1984), the Presidential Medal of Freedom (1996), and the International Freedom Conductor Award (1998).

Rosa at the 1999 ceremony where she was presented with the Congressional Gold Medal

Rosa Parks was the first woman and first non-government official to lie in honor in the Rotunda of the U.S. Capitol in Washington DC.

There have been other tributes to Rosa's courage as well. The city of Montgomery, Alabama, has named a street after her. Hundreds of other roads, schools, and parks around the country bear her name. The Smithsonian Institute in Washington DC displays a statue of Rosa. The Rosa Parks Library and Museum was founded at Troy University in Montgomery. It helps people understand the events that led to the famous bus boycott.

Rosa Parks died on October 25, 2005, at the age of 92. Throughout her life, she worked for equality and justice. She seemed to touch everyone she met, from children to senior citizens. Rosa believed that intelligence and self-respect are powerful weapons against **prejudice**. She is proof that the act of one person can change the world. Today, her life continues to inspire many people to demand equality.

Rosa sat in the front of a Montgomery bus on December 21, 1956, after the Supreme Court ordered the bus system to be integrated.

TIME LINE

1910   1920   1930–1949   1950

1913
Rosa McCauley is born in Tuskegee, Alabama, on February 4.

1918
Rosa starts school in Pine Level, Alabama.

1924
Rosa attends school in Montgomery, Alabama.

1929
Rosa leaves school to care for her grandmother.

1932
Rosa marries Raymond Parks.

1934
Rosa receives her high school diploma.

1943
Rosa joins the NAACP and is elected secretary of the Montgomery chapter.

1955
Rosa is arrested on December 1 for violating the bus segregation law.

1956
On February 21, Rosa is arrested a second time for participation in the Montgomery Bus Boycott.

1956
On November 13, the Supreme Court declares the laws requiring segregated buses to be illegal.

1957
Rosa and her family move to Detroit, Michigan.

1964
President Lyndon Johnson signs the Civil Rights Act on July 2.

1965
Rosa joins the staff of Representative John Conyers.

1977
Rosa's brother and husband, Raymond, both die of cancer.

1979
Rosa's mother dies.

1987
Rosa founds the Rosa and Raymond Parks Institute for Self Development.

1988
Rosa retires from John Conyers's staff.

1992
Rosa Parks: My Story is published.

1996
President Bill Clinton presents Rosa with the Presidential Medal of Freedom.

2000
The Rosa L. Parks Library and Museum opens at Troy University in Montgomery, Alabama.

2005
Rosa dies on October 25 at the age of 92.

GLOSSARY

appeal
(uh-peel)
Attempting to change a court's decision by asking a higher court to consider the case is called an appeal. Rosa challenged her court verdict with an appeal.

boycott
(boy-kot)
Not using a certain product or service as a form of protest is called a boycott. The Montgomery Bus Boycott protested segregation on Montgomery buses.

civil disobedience
(siv-ul diss-uh-bee-dee-uhns)
Civil disobedience is disobeying government laws in order to protest them. The Southern Christian Leadership Conference (SCLC) used civil disobedience to protest racism and discrimination.

civil rights movement
(siv-il rites moov-muhnt)
The struggle for equal rights for blacks in the United States during the 1950s and 1960s is often called the civil rights movement. Martin Luther King Jr. was a leader of the civil rights movement.

discrimination
(diss-krim-i-nay-shun)
Discrimination is unfair treatment of people based on differences of race, gender, religion, or culture. In the South during the 1950s, many whites participated in discrimination against blacks.

integrate
(in-tuh-grayt)
To combine different things together into one group is to integrate them. A goal of the Montgomery Bus Boycott was to end unfair treatment of blacks on Montgomery buses.

lynching
(linch-ing)
Lynching is putting a person to death by hanging without legal cause. In the South, the lynching of blacks was often a crime that went unpunished.

prejudice
(prej-uh-diss)
A negative feeling or opinion about someone without just cause is prejudice. Prejudice against blacks existed because of their skin color.

racism
(ray-sih-zum)
Racism is the belief that one race is superior to another. Rosa and other blacks experienced racism from whites.

segregation
(seg-ruh-gay-shun)
The act of keeping race, class, or ethnic groups apart is called segregation. Before the Supreme Court ruling against it, segregation was legal on Montgomery buses.

Underground Railroad
(un-dur-ground rayl-rohd)
The Underground Railroad was a network of people who helped blacks escape slavery before the U.S. Civil War. Through the Rosa and Raymond Parks Institute for Self Development, children can follow the path of slaves that escaped by the Underground Railroad.

verdict
(vur-dikt)
A verdict is a decision by a jury stating if a person is guilty or not guilty of a crime. At Rosa's first trial on December 5, 1955, she received a guilty verdict.

Further Information

Books

Bolden, Tonya. *Portraits of African-American Heroes*. New York: Penguin, 2005.

Freedman, Russell. *Freedom Walkers: The Story of the Montgomery Bus Boycott*. New York: Holiday House, 2006.

McNeese, Tim. *Civil Rights Movement: Striving for Justice*. New York: Chelsea House, 2007.

Parks, Rosa. *Rosa Parks: My Story*. With James Haskins. New York: Penguin, 1999.

Pastan, Amy. *Martin Luther King, Jr*. New York: DK Publishing, 2004.

Videos

Mighty Times: The Legacy of Rosa Parks. Dir. Robert Houston. Tell the Truth Production, 2002.

The Rosa Parks Story. Dir. Julie Dash. Xenon Pictures, 2002.

Web Sites

Visit our Web page for links about Rosa Parks:

http://www.childsworld.com/links

NOTE TO PARENTS, TEACHERS, AND LIBRARIANS: We routinely verify our Web links to make sure they are safe, active sites—so encourage your readers to check them out!

INDEX